POEMS OF MY NIGHT

Poems of My Night © 2016 by Cynthia Pelayo

Published by Raw Dog Screaming Press
Bowie, MD

First Edition

Cover illustration: Steven Archer
Book design: Jennifer Barnes

ISBN: 978-1-935738-88-6
Library of Congress Control Number: 2016953019

Printed in the United States of America

www.RawDogScreaming.com

POEMS OF MY NIGHT

CYNTHIA PELAYO

RAW DOG
SCREAMING
PRESS

To my father
Para mi Papa

Author's Note:

In the following poems I respond to poetry written by the great Jorge Luis Borges. Borges was born in Argentina in 1899, and was educated in Europe. His poetry, essays, and short fictions, known as ficciones, would go on to win worldwide acclaim, including his sharing the International Publisher's Prize with Samuel Beckett.

This book of poems is divided into two parts; the first is a response to each poem in *Poems of the Night*. These poems explore ideas of sleep, insomnia, meditations on death, and blindness – which Borges would later go on to suffer from. The second is a response to a collection of poems that appear in *Selected Poems*. Borges once said that poems came to him in his dreams, and that they were the gift of the night. Spending so much time with Borges has truly been a gift of its own.

Table of Contents

PRIMERO: POEMS OF THE NIGHT

Forjadura..15

Amanecer 16

Un patio...17

Calle con almacén rosado..18

Una despedida...19

Afterglow 20

Inscripcion sepulcral...21

Remordimiento por cualquier muerte 22

El general va en cocoche al muere 23

La noche que en el sur lo velaron 24

La noche de San Juan...25

Casa juicio final 26

Dreamtigers..27

Insomnio..28

La noche ciclica...29

Poema conjetural...30

Del infierno y del cielo..31

Museo 32

El poeta declara su nombradia..33

Poema de los dones 34

La luna...35

Arte poetica..37

Los espejos 38

Limites...39

El golem...40

Alguien...41

Donde se habran ido 42

El sueno 43

El sucida...44

Elegia 45

The unending rose 46

Ein traum...47
Signos 48
Endymion on Latmos 49
Ni siquiera soy polvoI 50
Un sabado 51
Adan es tu ceniza 52
Historia de la noche 53
La joven noche 54
Dos formas de insomnio 55
Poema 56
Yesterdays...57
El sueno 58
Los suenos..59
Un sueno...60
Alguien sonara..61
Sueno sonado en Edimburgo 62
El caballo 63
Una pesadilla..64
Doomsday...65
Midgarthormr 66
Inferno, V, 129...67
Elegia de un parque..68
Haiku..69
La cifra..70
Milonga del muerto 71
El don 72
Maestro...73

SECONDARIO: COLLECION DE POEMAS

El hacedor...76
Un dialogo sobre un dialogo 77
Espejos cubiertos..78
Argumentum ornithologicum 80
La cautiva...81
The plot...82
The witness..83

Amoras anticipation 84

Jactancia de quietud 85

Manuscrito hallado de un libro de Joseph Conrad 86

Adrogue 87

Una rosa amarilla 89

Mi vida entera...90

Sunset Over Villa Ortega 91

Las cosas..92

La pesadilla 93

El remordimiento...94

A un gato 95

Yo (I)..96

Elegia de un parque..97

Sala vacia...98

Curso de los recuerdos 99

No eres los otros...101

Los enigmas 102

A quien ya no es joven 103

El instante...104

El reloj de arena 105

Borges y yo..107

La lluvia 108

Mexico 109

El Borges 110

El Punal 111

Una brujula..112

A quien esta leyendome..113

A una moneda...114

Al hijo 115

Fragments from an Apocryphal Gospel 116

Nostalgia del presente..118

PRIMERO: POEMS OF THE NIGHT

Forjadura

The thought of blindness makes me drown

Water seeps in my nostrils and floods my eyes

Words have left me exposed to the sharpness of diseased night

The specs of light are fleeting still, perhaps fragmented dreams

All is a recurring nightmare, of that daytime things were pure – but will
never be again

Tears wrap their hands around my neck, digging into my flesh

The memory of summertime sidewalks burn my bare feet

I long for the feel of the cool alley asphalt against my toes

It is coming, this time I know

Anticipation makes it all the more violent

I'll take this heaviness and maybe one day the evening will strip it from my
shoulders

Only then will the diamond moon steal my cry

Amanecer

A cursed wind blew, shaking the trees, my windows, the street lights swayed
Disturbing the night, reminding the world that day crept forward with its
promises
Shadows lurched from their corners, angry at the great offense
I remembered a dream where I dreamt the world and it dreamt me
Was this more than just a reminder? Was the silence telling me it was time
to sleep, to dream the day?
Since I was awake unable to dream my day did this then make me an
insomniatic fool?
Were all of us who were awake right now tempting the Fates, defying our
obligation to end the night?
Our muddled minds together were hazards to the light
The threat of a forever night lingered and the darkened shapes watched me
while I watched them
Stepping away from the blinds I closed my eyes and wished for it to come,
just once more
Maybe another chance is what I needed
When I woke I silently cursed myself for constructing it all back together,
my house, the birds outside
the sun and the dirtied sidewalks on spotlight
Outside, an old man with a black cane walked passed my window
Suddenly, he stopped, turned and smiled at me like only a blind man could

Un patio

We didn't have a patio growing up
There was the front porch where we would sit all summer long, watching
  cars go by
Listening to the secrets of our neighbors
The backyard was a different place, a squared oasis in a concrete picture
The moon would make the sidewalk bordering our backyard glow
And I wondered about this magical place while in bed
The backyard ended and where it stopped our home began but that was
  the place
Of lounging in chairs under the cool blanketed evening, of my father's
  laughter and cigarette smoke
Brave fireflies who came to the city, to our yard to dance
I think of these things, think of that yard, and wonder if it will always
  remain with me at night

Calle con almacén rosado

Those faces are gone, the ones that stood at every corner of every day
They were the guardians of that park and this very street
This street I find myself which has riddled my dreams
The roads are so close here that I am suffocating with the memories of its years
There, on that corner stood a weeping willow but someone tore it down
A decade later a young man was shot and killed there, just steps from
    where that tree cried
There is the basketball court, sad and empty, rusted backboards no longer
    hold circled hope
Water fountains run dry here
Dreams were forged here as were prayers and curses
Right there was a wooden bench painted green and many years ago there
    sat my grandfather, watching all of us
He watches us now
The corner store's windows are covered in fluorescent yellow signs with
    bold pink letters
Cigarettes, Candy, Conversation, your neighborhood friend
My years were lost on this street, they melted down and flowed into the sewer
Let me know when you find them
The streets suffer with me and it plays the musical wailings of my life

Una despedida

We gave each other our farewells under the shade of the evening
A monstrous evening of deep blue water and solitude folds
Your eyes ignited the way and we embraced as the night looked on
Covered in our privacy we abandoned what it was we came here for
That instead we could relish in our desperate loneliness
You drove far that night and as I waited anxiety seeped into my skin and
  was captured
I am one of the moon, I told you that, but then you are the great scorpion
You even frightened Venus away that night
The thorned bushes stabbed at my ankles and I left traces of blood along
  my way to you
The constructed lights of the city dried my nerves so that I could see you
  this final night
Evening that I hold in memory of you, or us, but maybe what you made of me
I reached too far that I fell away from this
The light rejected you as it rejects me now
Night guided us
Guides us still

Afterglow

As soon as I wake the sun is dying
No matter what you believe that orb is the ultimate trickster
Making you promises that its brilliance will give you solace
It moves from you, slipping away and falling behind
With that final strip of light on the horizon the betrayal is clear
We choke down the acceptance of night
We are abandoned by the day and left to wander Dante's black forest
Thinking only of that glow which now bleeds on our minds
Maybe it will end as childhood dreams end
Maybe the sun is just an illusion and the night has been our constant

Inscripcion sepulcral

I felt like I should have known you but I didn't really know either of you
I suppose you both were farmers of some kind
I'm not really sure what of what kind
One of you raised animals
The other cut sugar cane
One of you I grew up with
You lived upstairs
Each day you sat beside that window
The other I only met twice beside that mountain
You were my favorite
I'm sorry I left you
You both were dead within months of one another
You are both buried on that land, where you both were born, where I was born
It's strange to think that I am you and that you were me
The daughters' daughter of an angry conquistador
The sons daughter of a Native
I wonder if my skin will ever grow thick and dark like leather
From working outside hours under the sun
I wonder if my eyes will grow blurry from staring outside of the window
Wondering where it is I am

Remordimiento por cualquier muerte

A reminded reminder of that what once was
We have forgotten that they were there once, and still hold form
Whispered names cringed through cracked stone and silence finds its home
You see we are ghouls but they have been baptized by the stars and
  liberated
Freedom from this life's curses of trivialities; work and play
The corpse is not an erased chalkboard for it is La Muerte
The dead stand with you, a hand rests on your shoulder
A cold kiss presses faith to your cheek
Eyes may not look upon its front steps
Feet may not walk the sidewalk toward the bodega
They think what you are thinking, right there
They sense what you are feeling, just then
We are afraid but they are redeemed
Taking from us the power of the day and the beauty of the night

El general va en cocoche al muere

I wonder what it would look like, a great funeral coach parading down
    Fullerton Avenue
Four black horses clopping down the street, drawing bullet hole ridden souls
Their terror and their fear beaming off the street would be a splendid thing
Mourners drenched in tears and desperate signs of forgotten redemption
We have endured hundreds of days and thousands of nights in this
    wilderness
Asking ourselves if the church has died, if the city has died, if we have died
We've brought ourselves here, to this purgatory of the streets
Now we are dead, on our feet and through this day
We are ghosts and we have come here to our Hell of the Inner City
Broken by God and Bloodless

La noche que en el sur lo velaron

A house on the South Side is opened until dawn
I'm unfamiliar with it and I don't believe I will ever see it again
A dizzying light awaits me as I reach its creaking wooden steps
The house has been wasted away by bad dreams and horrible nights

Pausing at the door I wonder if I'm ready to make this deathwatch
There are memories here, more varied and bright than the stars overhead,
    and we cannot see
They have been clouded by the summer heat and the city's gun smoke
The world is a lonelier place tonight

The house receives me as it has received so many over the years
Inside men and women are restrained to their seats in their tide of grief
Our own destinies are on pause for some time, unimportant now, and we
    wonder if they ever were
We speak things quietly, feeling our realities with a shared uselessness

I am saddened by what we've lost here
Lost with every good death
Their reading habits, their favorite pair of shoes
And we are all here to take part in this vigil wake
We are gathered here today to surround this being – the Dead Man
He is in good company and we will guard him this first night in death

We will miss this night, as we will miss his life
There will never be another memory like this
I stumble into the night, wiping away its sad breeze
The darkness guides me as I walk home, weary and forever in mourning

La noche de San Juan

Collect St. Johns' Wort this day to keep away the witches and evade their
    evil brew
High fires erupt over and above the ponds, rivers and lakes
For our sins are giving thanks six months before the Christ
Wood blisters under the heat, reds and golds splashed across the blue night
The earth smells of smoke and as it bleeds, we bleed
Darkness is wild and sweet here while we wait and listen
The sidewalks don't know that once they weren't sidewalks at all
This was all campo here, fields trampled by hope, but stolen by greed
All that is pushed aside as we wrap our arms around the forgotten
Luke 1:5-25 and this Holy Feast
Don't search for your rosary beads they've turned to dust

Casa juicio final

These city streets are more than my angels, they are my blessed demons
They've refrained from stabbing daggers into my back but instead have jammed
ice picks in my eyes forcing me never to blink
All I see is blood running and it runs now on cold, soulless asphalt
Where I've walked I've wondered if others have felt my anguish
These were steps I sat down on once to cry
The trembling you feel when you walk up those stairs are mine
This city has given me loneliness wrapped in wicked misery
I kiss her goodnight each night and each morning she embraces me with
   her rusted hope
We are a domestic abuse the two of us and she knows that I will not
   abandon her
I want to walk her nighttime city streets but she keeps me inside
Lions and cobras lurk behind parked cars and in dark alleyways
Sometimes you can see spray painted warnings begging intruders to turn away
"Here be dragons"
I'll wait until it is safe, which it will never be, but still I will never leave her

Dreamtigers

I must have been very young but I remember standing there
Beside the chain link fence of my red brick school and my father in the
  car waiting
That day, the bus would come to take me to see the tigers

Memories have faded, or melded, or been replaced by illusions since then
but I believe I saw them that day, the very first day, and they were sad as I
  was sad
Golden hair and limp muscle paced back and forth, eyes blinded by despair

I've thought of them since, and many nights and many days since I have
  visited them
Their dragging steps mimic my sadness and I only hope they understand
  my stillness
senses their Plexiglas covered pain

I've tried to dream with them, pulling them into my mind at night but
  something's not working
Maybe the zoo has erected a barrier that holds them there at night
  preventing them
from escaping even for a few hours into my safe dream world

Insomnio

Buses and trains run all night in this city, not all of them, but some of them
I've stayed awake standing on those platforms, watching them go by
A blur of people with midnight purposes serving as an instantaneous blur
You are why I cannot sleep

There are shouts from one corner and cries from an apartment window
They too cannot close their eyes and escape this night's reality
We did this to them, as I have done this to myself
One day I will be able to close my eyes and escape you all

There's so much steel and glass here
My dreams have been layered into the foundation and I have
walked those corridors begging for a remedy only to find myself looking
    down the stairwell
Below there is no sleep just darkness, and what purpose does darkness serve
    if there is no sleep?

Clouded mind and restless eyes
I've been abandoned too well and my mind is a fog of café con leche con azucar
because if I cannot rest then I must be fully awake and this is my evening
    of penance

La noche ciclica

In the future I will be here again. A woman who claimed to be a psychic once told me
that in my past life I was a photographer and in this life I was still learning what it was I had
failed to learn, and that I would return once more, as evidently reincarnation didn't serve me well

Sometimes I long for things as they once were. I should have taken their pictures but instead
fell fancy to the smell of a particular city street or the
hum of a certain street light. These are the things I will miss then

The city takes a breath without me and without me it constructs this idea, this grand plan of
change, of twisted corridors, locked gates and shuttered windows
I hope I will recognize this town then, although, it is familiar now as I am living it

This will all be repeated, you and I – you standing on that corner and me smiling, looking up at you
One day it will not be a matter of direction that keeps us from this meeting place, there will be no
North and South or East or West or pitiful subjugations

The minotaur will guard these things, our things, and he'll direct us, whether through fear
or through torment, and we'll repeat all of this; North, South, East, West, matters of rejections
standing on that corner, twisted corridors, grand plans, city street, certain breaths

I promise as this repeats I will take that picture

Poema conjetural

I've wondered about those fractions of moments and in fluttering thoughts
Death can be sensed some say. Death manipulates and adjusts the
temperature of a room
You see there – the lighting is softened so that your eyes will be
comfortable as they fall upon her
As she glides into the room with a spectral bouquet

The tragedy is that you have ignored her but she is always with you, a
whisper in your ear
We will all be there at our appointment with her one day
La Muerte, she has you on speed dial
Transportation is what matters and perhaps that is what we all dread

I've wondered about those who have died beneath the stars, encased in
moist earth
The stars, the final pleasant sight experienced, but then there are those
surrounded by
heat and smoke and the rotted smell of anger and despair
In that time and in that place they feel her approach

In that fraction of that moment do you panic with wonder or suffer with
question?
So much can change in a moment. Time could have tricked you into that
wood or onto that field
of bullets and terror. That car was not supposed to swerve left as you
swerved right
These decisions are made without your consent and here is your true tragedy

Del infierno y del cielo

At the entrance of the labyrinth the man whispered to himself "For the
elected there is Paradise. For the ejected there is the Inferno."

This is when he began his course, stepping into the very center. Instead of a
beastly minotaur awaiting the intruder with blood pasted on its mind, he
found God, pacing back and forth.

Then, the trumpet sounded. Neither of them was startled for they knew it
had been time.

He continued on, past corridors of hope and passages of tragedy.
There he saw destiny mangled and purity shattered.
Inconsistencies of direction made their way known as these things do.

Inferno was marked through the midway, a life of journey and an echoed
wooden path. Here he had wandered from the straight path. And at the
end the Shade told uttered "But you must journey down another road,"
and so the man did.

There, he found the heavens ablaze.
The sun rained down rivers of revelation.
Just fires of desires drowned.

This is the inverted pyramid.
Your time is your heaven, is your hell.

You are faithful still to yourself but you are not beyond corruption.

This semidarkness will not fade.

Museo

They are hung up here
Their dead are in the past now

There is Lichtenstein. There is Degas. There is Miró. There is Dali. There
is Warhol.
There is Matisse. There is Rembrant. There is Picasso. There is Manet.
There is Munch.
There are so many more

I fear they watch me in those cold hallways
I search glass for their reflections

This is not a place for faces but of distorted shapes

Perhaps I come here because I grow weary under these lights
And these forms remind me how much death has already used me up

El poeta declara su nombradia

My devices are charcoal and the night.
The inspiration is stored in dust covered tombs.
Though these histories are catalogued I'll reshape them, they're my clay.
The angels know my mind is never at rest and so they'll whisper in my ear.
White walls are covered in my smudged fingerprints.
I only hope to remain after death.

Poema de los dones

The burned pages of Alexandria have made it so that I can never experience scent
Serapeum, her sister, mourns and I suppose I mourn with her as well
Julius Caesar you've wasted so much but we seem to have forgotten the
    failures set alight by your ships
Caesar, I wonder if you read the manuscripts of Aeschylus, Sophocles, or
    Euripides. Did you dream them?

Those libraries were places I feared, intimidated by their stories, fearful of
    memories I could not take away
Blinded by those faded spines, gold leaf rubbed away by people I will never know
I wonder if they've thought of me, the reader whose fingers would replace
    theirs in the future
A part of them has been sealed within those pages as well as the print of my
    fingertips

Their corridors are quieter now, not for their purpose but because the
    people have fled
Minds have been broken by these other things, flitting things, with hollow
    moving parts
I've fought being lost like them for so long, for their purpose is not a
    purpose but a droning void
instead I'll make my way to those abandoned shelves to escape them

My dread continues, my fear is the exterior which allows me to slip inside
I've been dead at that entrance for a long time but still I'll wonder what
    more could have been done
The faded, mildewed galleries, the blank faces that fill no room
I'll stay silent so you can continue to sleep

La luna

There's this distinction beyond all others that the pale orb that hovers
above us
is an object positioned there by the gods to mark the path of our history
This disc is bolded by superstition and illuminates angels and their darkly
opposite
Our justification for it is the same across all cultures 'The moon made me
do it.'

For the Maya, she is the goddess of growth, as well as the conductor of
disease
Popol Vuh tells that two siblings were transformed into the sun and the
other the moon
Maybe she is patroness of Venus, connected to the jaguar god of the
underworld
Or, maybe it is sibling rivalry that punctuates our skies

That lunar being is not only white, but it can appear to us as golden rivers
of black and blue
Some nights it disappears behind the blanket of the universe, guarding its
shyness
Performing magic behind a cloud on a breathless night confident you'll
discover its indiscretion
When the thirteenth moon rises, and the sky is illuminated sapphire its
powers will grant your wish

Lycanthropy takes place nights of the Lunar Effect and many lock their
doors and windows
This Transylvania Hypothesis is based on no scientific reason but the belief
in deviant behavior
Nights of this wicked moon remain in light levels throughout our world
Lunatic is Luna and can be found in the writings of Babylon

This celestial object has been our literary master to extend our words further

To set the setting, to explain our infinite strangeness, to design our fate
destined under black skies

It's a puzzle, that beaming sphere in the sky man has attempted for
millennia to understand

To demand why it shines down upon us in mockery while the remainder of
the sky has fallen to darkness

Arte poetica

Not only do silent rivers and lakes provide reflection
Nor do mirrors in your crumbling, dust-covered home
You are your own symbol of distorted illumination
Weeping madness is not easily forgotten

La Oreja de Van Gogh is tortured flesh ripped from the artist
Munch suffered as well from his father's seeds of madness
Stains that will not be scrubbed away by the supreme Fates
Only words or a blood-stained brush can alleviate the sting
There are times when we can walk outside among others
Pleased we have blended Edward Hyde within the crowd
We don't need a serum to become possessed
Our metamorphosis is involuntary

Murmurs are flitting and the images meant to dilute
Our meaning does not sustain our transformation
Darker impulses need more to cease
Death is beauty in poetry

Cynthia Pelayo

Los espejos

Curious pots of collected dark standing water
Marveled by smooth, polished obsidian
Sidon gave the coated glass of Turkey
A thin sheet of silver now coats our eyes

In the mirrored world another reality exists
Those people that pass in our moments
Sharing our realities, fixated upon us
Away, into their own cold foundations

Their movements are repeated in shadows
Slipping out of their cage, they walk among us
Manifesting within our homes as creaking doors
Tapping windows that cause violent sleep

Never trust who you seek in that cold glass
They're more than you, a measure of things
Of moments and meanings meant to disrupt
The balances of this eternal life unraveling
Take care as you sit and stare

Limites

There is a street you have walked down many times
You will never travel down this road again
Friends you have hugged months ago
Familiar eyes escape your memory

Voices that once were so familiar to you fade
Fabric taut to its limits has ripped through
Sadness is not knowing those moments
You will fail to never live them again

Everyday strangers become your friends
Days heralded when they no longer pass
Abandoned seats on the train mark loss
Life is continuous; loss and tragedy expected

Days were crowned by smiles were never
Failures to recapture memories tortured
Streets have changed, mapped in oddity
People have left, escaped with your moments

El golem

I visited Judah Loew ben Bezalel's synagogue at night as I walked to the
   Old Cemetery
I recall the cobble stone streets of Prague, how people watched me curiously
while I looked up at the window, shielded in shadows, fighting an urge to shout
above for whatever essence remained to come to the glass and find me

Created with the intent of defense, there is an element of sadness there
knowing you were not created to love but to destroy and your very existence
is sacrilege and man screams terrors to God when he sees your face molded
   of clay
your hurried anthropomorphic form given an empty life to be controlled

You were birthed in secrecy, your laboratory can be found in nightly words
whispers of the tower, and your home was destined to be that Ghetto
Do you ever walk to that window? Are you pacing those floorboards even now?
Or, were you really abandoned by your father in guilted mourning?

Those letters rest upon your forehead still and the syllables can easily be uttered
Golem, my unshaped form, you are unfinished before God's eyes
Developed with the esoteric secrets that gave us our ancestor Adam
Your sleep is not truth in death

Alguien

A man who holds anger closely at his chest for fear that it will be dropped
A man who has remained seated far too many hours in a cold, cluttered room
A man who is bewildered by what he becomes when the crowd has formed
Who has learned where the lies are hidden within concentrated apologies
This man rejoices for oblivion exists easily beyond the reaches of his door
Aware that clatters flow in from outside and these are the calls of
    frameless humanity
Volcanic states of purified blood mixed with the echoes of fear drive some
    motivation
Delicate fury rides sustained designs of wretchedness

There's no reasoning or understanding of monsters developed from our
    own design
He knows to ignore the very glimmers of humility and reads you all as specimens
Mysterious happiness falls not for recollections of kindness for none exist
Gleeful demons encircle him, these are his children

Cries are the product of his success and sobs are the additional rewards
Searching for him is as simple as not recognizing him at all
One can never prophesize their own killer

Donde se habran ido

They've faded away, and were pressed in between two pages like a moth
Cells have dried and deteriorated without the notice of these caretakers
Remnants of their ghosts are marched through staged parade routes
Smiles are wooden, applauses are orchestrated, you have all forgotten
Music once blared on the battlefields, trumpeted drums and banners waved
Tunes roared as tears were halted by blows and bludgeoned wounds
Fall, winter, summer grasses drowned in the rust-colored life of men who
    cried for their home
Later the terrain changed, the purpose shifted, irrational reasons expounded

At night the jungles swell with regret and the fog that floats above the tree line
remembers the rips, the screams, the terrified starving faces who were trapped
in their home, their hell, these landscapes created centuries before as their coffins
Stars watch hidden remains tucked behind trees, tunnels, and buried in
    deserts and beyond

Valor is the emotion that stings while bravery is the ingredient the gods
    added to their
blood, blazoned their hearts with steel and lifted their souls to pedestals
For both sides have reasoned with their losses and sustained their defeat
Where have they gone, the true valiant warriors who are meant to conquer
    cruelty?

El sueno

We open to a chapter in progress, a play in media res
The masquerade ball at Prince Prospero's castle
Where I have danced with nobles and Red Death
The next act is tragedy, of Ophelia's plot
And graveyard conversation with Hamlet
There's incessant sweeping and midnight snatches
Me into the in between of wake and sleep paralysis
Shadows stand at the foot of my bed and clawed
Attempts fail and I'm followed by unknown faces
The dead sit with me and tell me their regrets
Regret comes to me, repeated obsessions
Night rolls this way, cyclical inescapable horrors

El sucida

I sit at the Office of the Parting Soul From the Body
I've turned my face away from sin only to be drenched in it by others
Unto the wicked there shall be nightmares of my time
Leaving with nothing is easy as I am the burden to bear
No one will ask for my ashes for fear they will stain
The mistake is thought contagious, you're my ashes to ashes
I'll listen to no reason and I'll walk away from the last sunset
Don't be troubled for I'll leave nothing to the memory of me

Elegia

There are three faces I think of, the first is the Northern Star, believed
    positioned directly overhead, but it burned out long before
The other is the horizon, that shadowy line that divides the Earth from the
    setting sun, but we never see its true form
The final face I think of is Death, how sacred she is and how her pillar
    stands above that of
God and the Devil
My guilt as well will pass, but until then, I will stay shrouded in your ignorance
Past the curtains, I'll give you praise to your forever farewell
We pass Phlegethon, Acheron, Cocytus, and Styx. The great marsh
    underground visited by Dante.
Charon will ferry you, ignoring the wrathful and sullen, and those drowned
    in muddy waters
I think of them, the new souls. I pray for the old souls, those forgotten
    shades, faces printed on paper long faded, identities and lives lost in
    news reports and police files
I'll think of those bodies, unceremoniously submerged in oceans, rivers and lakes
At night, I'll pray silently for those laid to rest in forests and dumpsters
I think of those smothered in their cries. I think of those blasted for street
    names, corners, and color
I think of my own death, how many of them will not know when I pass,
    how my name will fall from no one's lips and how my grave will one day
    be a pathetic garden path, as anonymous as all of the others.

The unending rose

On Saint George's Day I will think of the Virolai
I'll pray for those dark red roses, the gifts between empty lovers
I listen to the words of the hymn and as I sing I can see her
Rosa d'abril, Morena de la Serra
A rose in April. The dusky lady
The wonderful lady of that majestic mountain chain
I remember you handed me a rose in Barcelona, on Las Ramblas
Catalonian sun burned and I cried
Columbus returned from his tortuous voyage
The Nina, the Pinta, the Santa Maria
They floated on luck and smelled of blood
The petals were kept, to be folded in a Bible,
Slipped from my hand and fell in the street.
They browned and withered and I wonder now
Can you hear that angelic song?
Before you speak secrets, listen
Place a rose above the door
Keep it in your heart, *Sub Rosa*
The Virgin is secured in stone at Montserrat
Can she hear the singing?
Encased in glass
Thorns grow, reaching for the mountain
Serving as her prison
It's the mystery of infinity
How red velvet can easily slip from its base and die by your touch

Ein traum

I met Kafka at the Prague astronomical clock at midnight
We looked up at the four figures;
Vanity, the Miser with his bag of gold, the Turk and Death rang his bell
    and I awoke alone.
I met Vanity at the Prague astronomical clock at three o'clock in the
    afternoon
She asked me where I had left my friend, the man who dreams of me.
When I turned to answer her
She was Death and she rang her bell
I met the Miser at the Prague astronomical clock at nine o'clock in the evening
He told me his bag of gold weighed him down.
He gave me two coins and told me to cover the eyes of the man who dreams
When I opened my mouth and asked if he spoke of Kafka, the Miser rang
    his bell
It was three o'clock in the morning and I met the Turk at the Prague
    astronomical clock
We stood in silence, listening to Death's bell.
We watched the doorway above the clock
The twelve apostles paraded through.
"He dreams of you," the Turk whispered at the end of the procession.
When I awoke, Kafka was there and it was midnight and we were at the
    Prague astronomical clock

Signos

IN THIS HOUSE LIVED EDGAR ALLAN POE
The rectangular bronze plaque was obscured by curious gawkers
Jeans and t-shirts blocked wooden trimmed doorways
The first room, suffocated by tourist cameras, snapped pictures of a once
was kitchen
Horse-hair plaster and whitewashed walls
The second room, the sitting room, or parlor, where a fire once cracked
ached under the footsteps of strangers
The narrow stairway squeezed my ribs until I found myself between two
rooms
Bedroom 1, believed to be Edgar's
Bedroom 2, believed to be Virginia's and Maria Clemm's
Lungs were crushed as I stepped up the narrow winding steps that peaked
into the small third floor room, where dying grandmother lay
Heavy burdens once hung here, promises burned away in brick hearths
Outside thousands of ravens cawed in lots littered with empty snack bags
and beer bottles
Bare branched trees nestled these birds of yore who sat in perpetual vigil
Row house glory crumpled under government housing
Memory holds the 2 ½ story duplex together

Endymion on Latmos

The twin gods were born on the island of Delos
God of sun and goddess of the moon
Your birthplace has thus been purified
The land purged, bodies dug up and removed
No mother will ever birth new life here
Or, was that the island of Paximadia
The Libyan Sea appears to me in Odyssey
I'm weak and so I'll sleep to dream of her
To dream of her and so I'll lay down to sleep
Celestial and divine, and inaccessible to all
My mortal skin longs to be in your infinite presence
They'll flee from me, because they find horror
In my nighttime secrets slipped under temples
Your Sacred Lake has been left to dry
Artemis of the Wild land, Mother of Animals
Holy Cypress trees find comfort in your name
I'll tell you of my solitude tonight and I'll sing to
You things of spirits and myth and we'll find Zeus

Ni siquiera soy polvoI

I am here and did not ask to be. This is my misfortune.
I've been handed twenty first century, *Anno Domini.*
Remnants of Canary Island dust and the African sun
Much of it has been the same as it was, but differently so
There were the towns and the squares, cobblestoned echoes
My years are meant to make up for the time those who could not be
The young woman who hemorrhaged to death on the farm floor
The kidnapped twin, horse prints on the mountain bid his farewell
The mother who sold her future in blustering factories
My idol is Saint Sebastian, tied to a post, pierced with Diocletian's arrows
At night, I reread Christopher Columbus' Requerimiento
King and Queen of Castile and Leon said we "shall make war against you"
And so, they took your wives and took your children and made slaves of them
For five hundred years my Borinquen bled
Then you gave me Jones Act and called me free
Then you gave me Operation Bootstrap and put me to work
The mainland didn't allow us to call her home
We sang in steel cars of our palm tree lined port
We felt bites of hounds and blasts of water cannons on Division Street
Nights were terrors of New Worlds unfounded
I'm no good as dust, and you'll never dream of me

Un sabado

The man shuffles through his worn house
Thirty-years of dreams and misery run through its pipes
Floorboards creak with the laughter of children
Windows rattled with a wind that sounds like his footsteps
The front steps paraded their grand possibility
Coffee brews on the counter, a stained porcelain cup awaits
Morning has not yet entered the day. There's still too much night for that.
He stands at the kitchen door, looking through the porch, outside
He has forgotten what it's like to see with both eyes
Regret clouds his retina, but the coffee is strong
The sip burns his tongue before he can utter an apology

Adan es tu ceniza

Bone of my bones and flesh and my flesh
The dust from which you originated cursed
Death passed upon all of us because your sin
Adam you were sent to al-Safa, Eve to al-Marwah
He wept for 40 days, and was then forgiven
God asked the angels to bow to you,
Iblis refused, for he was made of pure fire
We made the evil ones friends
The Devil breathes his evil intentions into your chest
Jinn speak wicked motivations in your ear as you sleep
God threw this disgraced angel away
Man's assault will come from before, behind, the left and right
Satan awaits you on your straight way

Historia de la noche

The Aztecs watched the parade of the Black Sun to its abyss
Itzpapalotl, the Obsidian Butterfly, crunched on bones during the solar eclipse
The entrance to the underworld's first layer is here on Earth
Walk into the mouth of the serpent and begin your descent
The path is lined with bioluminescent bones left behind by Tzitzimimeh
Our female demons dance for their stars, their skirts rattle with skulls and
   crossbones
Xolotl, will guard the sun on its journey below.
He will aid you through your challenges.
Rivers of blood are guarded by jaguars
The mountains will crash, and knives will race through the fields
Beasts await your heart, and the narrow passage between sharp cliffs
Will bring you to your darkness and rest
Souls of the dead can be found to the far North, in Mictlan
King Mictlantecuhtli and his wife Queen Mictecacihuatl will greet you
The Tzitzimimeh, our female demons, they'll dance for your end

La joven noche

Goethe presented me with his rose
Thorns broke skin, and blood ran down my wrist
Becoming petals singed with the words
Everything near becomes far
Don't trust the twilight, intentions shift in the night's luster
She ignores time. She copies the fiction of things.
The mirror hangs in her cellar, draped in the idea of gardens
Reflections of ancient norms and wandering ideas escape the image
Age spots on her hands burn. Wrinkles of worry scar her face.
The young night cannot be repeated

Dos formas de insomnio

What is insomnia?

It is lying awake, sensing the minutes pass. Only a few hours remain between you and the day. It's attempting to lie still, to forget, or more so, to ignore the failures of the previous day and the terrors of the new day approaching. It's the heaviness of your own body as it attempts to manage anxiety, through breaths forced to relax and tense muscles shifting to find a comfortable position, which does not exist. It is closing your eyes tightly, your mind telling yourself, demanding yourself to fall asleep, to let go and be taken away elsewhere. It's feverish, this desperation to want to sleep, to want to calm your mind, to force your body to behave in a way it will not because thoughts cannot slow. It is examining the noises around you, floorboards settling, walls shifting, faucets that drip with final drops from a glass of water poured. It is questioning shadows at the foot of your bed, streaks of light that splash across the walls as automobiles drive past your home of restlessness. It is guilt knowing that your body has failed you. That sickness will set in with this diseased lack of sleep. It's the day which mocks your failure to rest.

What is longevity?

It's in knowing that I have died slowly each day, ignoring the inevitability of death and thinking somehow I can elude it. It's in recognizing the failures I have hoped to forget, to erase from my mind with alcohol and sleeplessness, and burned letters, deleted accounts, and abandoned relationships. It's in referencing recent events only to be corrected that they were years ago. It's in forgetting, and knowing that my mind will fail me, is failing me and that others will one day triumph against me. It's in knowing that this sliver of time we are given is wretched because of its brevity. It's carrying a weight of conquest in my blood and knowing that I'll never know where I originated. It's in hating my story, because I was bred of hate, that crossed an ocean. My name, my language, my religion, it's not even mine. It's a Castilian I do not know how to speak. It's in wanting to remember what was lost across that ocean. It's in knowing that I will sink to my own death and I would have never really known what I was.

Poema

OBVERSE

Virgin, I'll ask for your twelve hexameters
The Aenid should have been burned, buried with you as you wished
In poetry, we don't always receive what we ask.
Your work, Eclogues 4, speaks of the birth of a boy heralded as the "great
    increase of Jove"
Was this Octavian, Julius Cesar's young heir, or did you speak of another?
Names can purify the relationship with the moon
Our natural elements spread across the atlas
Burn sandalwood for your protection and healing
Dante has arrived. Please escort him.

REVERSE

To wake someone from sleep is to deny them of respite
You have dissolved their universe
Destroyed their escape
Broken a sunset and cracked their dawn
True evil exists in the birth of a new day
Plans for the night's misdeeds are written under the sun
The night is its victim
Have you ever seen an old man cry to return to sleep?
Some of us live in our dreams

Yesterdays

A merchant and a man bound
And native chiefs and queens
Each fought and left their blood in the dirt
The battle waged and the other side had never known a weapon
These are the things my father does not want to hear
Victories of thievery
Pages celebrate the victor and blot the names of the kingdoms

El sueno

For those that do not believe in magic
I will talk to you of the night
It unravels the day's blemishes
And stirs them into amnesia
You are not who you are when you sleep
The night will gift you with all the things
You long to forget; escape from ever all
Burn your tears, and forget your blood
These walls and this floor walked over
And those whose steps I have trampled
I don't need to be them when I lay down
When the sheets grow cool and the sea
Changes and I don't have to listen
Ice forms over my lenses and that conquest
The name of Christopher, or was it Hernan?
None of them matter now, because I have forgotten
It all, when I have taken up a cross, and drank back
Wine

Los suenos

I don't dream of the future. I don't know of things of tomorrow, nor care. My dreams are of the past, conversations with the dead. Why would I dream of the living, when the dead long so much for me? We talk of the snow, and how it never ends here, and how the ice kills, but it won't kill me, even though I'm sure of it. The dead watch me in my dream, as I tilt my head up. The sky of my dream is a winter sky, grey and dead, penetrated by a wall of crystal. The dead won't touch me in my dream, they'll only look to my hands, wondering what it's like to touch the hand of a dreaming woman. I can't hear them, but I know what they're saying, that I should go and I should stop worrying, and pulling, tugging at a time that cannot reemerge from the depths of viscous time. I don't listen. What do the dead know after all? My eyes don't seem to function too well in the day, colors are no longer vivid and the world has taken on this haze, it's fading. Colors are bleeding. Objects have been stretched so far that they are no longer the things they should have been, and that's why the dead are there I wonder, but then I dream of me, sitting with the dead, watching them watching my hands, and I'm far away, in a dream in the present hues distorted. When I cross State Street I know my father will be there waiting for me. There are things he'd like to say, about this cold city, and how it's the city where I belong, because it will chill my marrow. Harsh voices from the train won't harm us. Rail road tracks underground are always on fire. None of this means anything, because I dream of him as he dreams of me.

Un sueno

Zoroaster whispered his vision to Queen Hutosa. She then told him of her
   dream.

A spiral stairway wound up a windowless, doorless tower. At the top of the
structure there was a single room. Inside this room sat a young woman,
her head bowed, long dark hair rested on her shoulders. Her face engaged
with the page before her and a pencil held steadily in her hand. She wrote
furiously. The markings on the page made panicked scratching sounds.
This movement was her breath. When Zoroaster asked Queen Hutosa what
this woman in the tower wrote the Queen replied "Of another woman, in
another tower, in another place, but at the same time."

Alguien sonara

I am dreaming of you, as you are now dreaming of me. Wouldn't it be freeing to release this world of slumber and night? To open our eyes and escape the construct of our body, skin and tendons. These bones are now part of the stars. When I wake I dream again, a revolving cycle of ellipses and I try to think, but I cannot recall what it was that Poe said about dreams? Are we nothing? Or, are we in a web? Are we all..? I cannot recall. Visions escape me and I can't grasp because a voice tells me to wake but the same voice instructs me to sleep and do you hear that? The bird is sleeping and I am asleep.

Sueno sonado en Edimburgo

And it begins like this.

Your ancestors summon you to a room. Let's say you received an invitation in the mail last Thursday. Across the top of the envelope the words "On the morrow" are written. That is the date you are expected to arrive at the location written on the index card in the envelope. Let's say that the location is given in a cipher. The colors are green, red, yellow and purple, with an absence of primary justifications. At a designated time, before the morning, after the sunset, and near the twilight you find yourself seated in the center of a vast warehouse. All along the walls are shelves. The shelves are empty. A man who indicates he his your ancestor is there. He asks you what you would like to fill those shelves with. You are not sure how to answer. You give him an answer, one answer. Your ancestor says you have answered incorrectly, that those letters have not yet been written. You are asked to read an unfamiliar language, written across a black chalkboard the height of a man. The words are blurred, sharp, linear. Somewhere in your memory you pull a night in Edinburg. The rain, a fine mist coats your face. You are walking down from the Crags heading toward the Royal Mile. The castle on the rock looks different in this light, your ancestor says when you approach the gate. Your past is unrecognizable.

El caballo

It was my first time there, on the island. It was an unexpected prison and you locked me in a humid room. From the room I could see the young boys outside and they looked so different, so unlike my complicated steel. It was the first time I had seen those creatures, golden horses. I pictured myself riding them, and I pictured it so strongly that I then found myself with those boys, and they were sweet and kind and so unlike all of my complications and I wanted to be like them, to smile like them, to beam like their souls. When they took me to their great horse the animal flared its nostrils and its eyes blazed. It did not want me then, nor needs me now.

Una pesadilla

I got off the bus, and felt as though someone got off just behind me. They were so close I could almost touch the fabric of their coat as my arms swung back in my walk. I was afraid to turn around, fearing they would ask why it was I was turning around and so I increased my step, and in turn the sensation of someone walking behind me quickly increased. The steps to my house were there, in sight, and I hurried, and those footsteps behind me hurried, and when I placed my hand on the gate I was sure to turn around this time, to close the gate securely and to see that there was no one there following me. I was greeted by the wind and parked cars and the debris that had blown onto my street from other streets in this other city. And so I walked up the steps to my door, and I inserted the key. That is when I heard the cough, it was not a cough of illness but a cough that indicated I should be aware that there was someone there, waiting for me to turn around and acknowledge their presence. He stood larger than all other men, and when he smiled I saw his teeth were razors. Markings covered his body, infinite tattoos that curled down his fingers and spiraled around his eyes. His smile was a glow of menace. This being was the nightmare of all things. His eyes turned downward, inspecting the locked gate. He nodded just once, tipped his hat and continued down his way.

Doomsday

Atomic plumes of mushroomed smoke
Silver coins in exchange for the location of the Son of Man
A pre-Columbian calendar ends
A Columbian arrives
The Great North Road ends and the pox spreads
Quetzacoatl was seen on the shore, sitting atop great beasts
A rooster crowed three times and Mary cried

Midgarthormr

Ouroboros, cyclical, recreating, reimagining, reenvisioning

Errors reawakened, the dead reborn. Singed Phoenix plumes regenerate anew.

Tutankhamun was read your story, and in it the god Ra completes his
union with Osiris in the Underworld. Serpents feast on their tails as
they'll feast on your wishes disguised in hopes.

Covered in night, you're protected in the abyss where the Shades cannot
reach you

Otherworldly disorder maintains the text written by Plato; the living, the
universe, the immortal, All created from the mythological entities that
align the maneuvers

Eyes are not needed to see as ears are not required to hear. The knowledge
is in the knowing and the moments dotted throughout the universe are
repeating themselves now

Wars will sweep open the curtains

Wolves will applaud the cast

Nothing is your nightmare

Inferno, V, 129

Alejandro waved to Rachel from the third floor window

He would wait there for her, at 6 in the morning and one morning

He wasn't there, standing, waiting

The building remains, red brick senior high school and he is now

Someone else with someone else raising someone else

But she still passes by that school, the buildings, the red bricks she wonders
   if they remember her

Sometimes, she walks by purposefully and sees the memory of him
   standing there

Waving at her, smiling at her, those black eyebrows, and that pleasant high
   school smirk

And sometimes she is her, that teenage girl whose heart would ache with
   joy all for a wave

She thought would be eternal

Elegia de un parque

This is life and we are living it now
Memories of tomorrow are entwined
With the decisions made yesterday
Positioned each stone illuminating the way
We are a reflection, instructed
Creation by the time makers
If this is now, then when is then?
There is no replicating a moment
There is difficulty remembering
Exact moments of worn memories
Indistinguishable facts refuted
Your case number documented
Analogous riddles and ephemeral waste
You serve as a mirror to those waiting
You'll dance in the park, waiting to return
Greet yourself in the landscape of forever

Haiku

I cried in my dream
Night was muddled by afterthoughts
Regrets are my nightmares

Exhaustion spikes when the eyes rapidly move
Guilt lays on my pillow
Your promises cover me in blankets

At midnight I hear your voice
I'm blinded by your memory of me
We've both aged and yesterday dissolved

Time should be hated
When it lies to us at dawn
Promises are ripped from our lips

Tree limbs hang low
Evergreens smell of embalming fluid
My fingers sign over oblivion

I died but no one knew
My casket was covered in rain
And my bones find shelter with no one

La cifra

You sat there in the train station telling yourself that you would be back
Next time you would spend more time, and speak to more people and talk
more of things
A new train enters the station and new people get off
Some of them look like people you may talk to one day soon
Others look like ghosts from your recent memory
You smile at one of them, a woman with a maroon skirt
With her head bowed she walks swiftly past you and you wonder if she's
just a
Residual haunting, repeating on this frequency until eternity ends or limits
stretch
The ticket in your hand tells you a time and a date, and its neither close to
the time or the date
You continue to sit there, waiting for the woman in the maroon skirt

Milonga del muerto

I stole holy water from the church
The bottle is hidden under my chair
I'll use it, splashing it on my cheeks when
Gabriel blows his horn

The sea to me is a tragic place
Where stolen people leaped into the waves
Flesh and bone shimmer in the water
Later, I'll tell you the rest

On a hilltop our house sat
It was taken, of course
Coffee beans, and banana plants paid for others
The jungle stole my grandfather's home

We were told we needed to fight
We were told we needed to stop breeding
We were told we were whores
We were told we weren't men

Great care is taken to act with discretion
Talking to ourselves, instructions to fit
A cross is burned into my feet
Psalms I will not forget

My blood is made of their blood and I am
The bastard child of a hundred slaves
The mistress of a thousand conquistadors
And the lone princess who bled for her island

Cynthia Pelayo

El don

The blind man entered the tent
The woman held up her mirror
The glass allowed him to see
Only his face and only for a moment
In this moment he regarded lines, and curves
Grey eyes and a wrinkled forehead
Behind himself he saw another man
Entering the tent
When he turned he found himself
Blind and distracted by the things he wanted to see
But never seeing the infinity before him

Maestro

Grand Maestro, I'll call you this, right now in hopes that you hear me. I'll send my prayer to you, through dream dusted night, sprinkled with true nightly terrors that we'll never repeat to the living. Walls have stopped me from dictating this word, this single word if uttered will lead the minotaur to me. Beasts kill savagely, poetically. This violence is in the nature of the labyrinthine world. Some nights I wake myself in a panic, finding myself in a darkened room and that second before my eyes adjust to the darkness I wonder if I have gone blind and I slip into the reasoning of navigating the seas without the sun's reflection. It's either my panic, my eyes, or the patron saints that give return to me the pity of sight. Will they ever one day forget to return it? You can suffocate with oxygen. You can drown without water. His footsteps are growing closer now, the bull-headed creature sent to destroy me for my vision. Part man. Part bull. Dante found him in his inferno, this monster whose entire zone is violence. His shadow creeps upon the wall now. Horns peak behind the curtain. Raging black eyes find victory in this, my fear. I call upon my saint, my savior, my only hope for survival. "I beg you to please come save me. Come find me, Borges!"

SECONDARIO: COLLECION DE POEMAS

El hacedor

I enter your office. You're reading a book. I can't see the title, nor the words, but I know there is text on the page. Behind you are seven stacks of books, each stack has an equal amount of books. Each stack is also identical in height, alignment and color. The binding is exact across each spine so that the gold leaf is uniform. The titles are obscured. My vision is failing me. Your head is lowered, and you make the slightest of movements as your eyes divert from one page to the other. Your hair is white, a crystalline white, the white of glaciers. You murmur something. It sounds like "Argentine," but it could be "Seraphim." Your right hand rises, takes the top right hand corner from the page and turns it over. You are now on the last page. I'm not sure what number that page is, but I'm sure that each volume behind you contains that same number somewhere within its pages. You take a deep breath. Your shoulders relax. You have discovered the villain. You have resolved the crime. Your protagonist will live in their happily ever after, contained within their infinite pages. You place your hands on the table, and slowly you rise, still looking downward at the final page. Eyes are settled on those final obscured words. "Listen," you say. "The pages are thinking of what to write next." Your eyes closed and your face is serene as your mind tells the pages where they should go next. Opening your eyes you place your hands on the book, closing it slowly, making sure no sound comes crashing from the pages. Delicately, you take the book to the closest stack where you place it. Again, each stack is even, containing the same number of books, same height, and same alignment. You turn back to your desk and sit down at your seat. Again, another book appears before you. Carefully, you turn the hardcover, and you begin, reading your words as they are written.

Un dialogo sobre un dialogo

A. What if we're all demons? Where's the purity then? Guillermo Garcia lit his cigar in front of me in defiance. Four people we've known in these short decades of our lives have died by suffocation, their lungs growing putrid from their youthful decisions. I prefer the night. I prefer the ubiquitous fear. When we acknowledge that we know nothing and can give way to despair then we are free. Cemeteries have become this museum to the dead. Everyone knows they exist but no one seeks them out for a visit. Cremation has become the preferred way to mourn and hide our dead. We should embrace the spectacle of death. Dying is the feast, but the event is in our dying. All brave men die. Perhaps we should continue to sit here, to welcome the eternal. Then we can be embraced in the glory of a good and welcomed death. Or, perhaps we should kill ourselves, Guillermo, so that we can continue this discussion elsewhere.

Z. You will always reconsider.

A. I don't recall what we said that night before. The gales drown out the sound. Perhaps we committed suicide that morning.

Espejos cubiertos

Mohammed ben Al-Ahmar recognized the beauty of the ruins of the small fortress built in 889 and largely forgotten until his arrival in the 11th century. The palace built with quadrangular plans was reconstructed as the pearl set in emeralds for the last Emirs of Spain. With the Andalusian mountains as the backdrop, the architects designed rooms that opened out into the central courtyard. Each room was built with the same principle, each connected by smaller rooms and passages. The sun and wind entered freely and the outside, while plain, protected the arabesque behind the walls. Rhythmic lines, scrolls and interlacing foliage and tendrils burst into careful decorative art that presented no figures, for figures were the construct of God. The sound of fountains and running water lead to the reflecting pools. The overgrown wildflowers, roses, and myrtles framed me in my reflection and I shuddered. My earliest memory looking into a mirror was that of my piercing, horrid screams. It was night, and then I entered the bathroom and turned on the light to look in the mirror and the image I found was darkness. Ever since that moment I have tried to avoid these pools of glass where night is trapped. My face in each mirror is deformed and strange, my demon self. When I look into the mirror, I know that is the place where the demons can follow me, hopping from mirrored place to mirrored place to mock me in my despair. Calling for help to my God and to my guardian angels as I peer into the glass is useless, the mirror blinds heavenly eyes.

My mother feared this madness and in thinking she was going to cure me instead scarred me. She set a mirror at the wall, directly in front of my bed. Once the lights went out sleep would not come because I could hear the tyrants at the mirrored gate breathing.

After one unpleasant night, I smashed the mirror with my bare fists, leading to several dozen stitches and mother accepted my mania.

It took some time, but as an adolescent I ignored mirrors. As an adult I made do, learning to shave without the use of reflection. Driving never turned into a reality for me, because of the required mirrored utilities. And so, I continued this way, avoiding myself, avoiding my reflection, and avoiding the whispers for so much time, until I met a woman. She loved me and I loved her and so we married. She accepted my fears, and when we had a daughter she never thought, nor I, that the curse would continue. Her name was Sylvia, and each time the child looked into a mirror she too would utter a horrendous scream. When she turned five, she accidentally locked herself in the bathroom, and the full length mirror tortured the girl. After the door was broken in we found her laying on the floor, a shard of glass in her hand and the mangled, blooded injuries she had inflicted to her eyes and ears. "Those things," my young daughter cried. "I couldn't look at them, nor listen to them anymore. They were you, your demons."

Argumentum ornithologicum

I don't need to close my eyes because they're always there, the crows. I looked out of my hospital window and I saw them, the crows. It's difficult to recall how many crows there were. I wondered if I had dreamed them, their black plumes, and their sharp beaks that shined like black stones. When I tried to remember the number I became stuck in this loop; are they definite or indefinite? And if so, does God know how many birds I encountered? If God exists, then is the number indefinite because he would have counted. If I had seen lesser crows, say, I had seen fewer than ten crows, but there was at least one, but I did not see four, nor, three, nor two crows. I saw a number between four and one, more than a murder or less than an attempt? It's difficult to say for certain. Or, was it ten? Did I see a number between ten and one? An integer of not nine, and not eight, not seven, nor six, or five, and so on. Is it all inconceivable that something exists?

La cautiva

Ernesto Mendoza has a nervous tic. His left leg, crossed over his right shakes. He catches the movement when the man seated directly across from him, from behind a desk raises an eyebrow. Mendoza unfolds the left leg, bringing it down to the floor, both feet planted firmly. Across from him four men are seated and one woman at a table. Each has a computer opened in front of them. Mendoza remembers when these things were done with paper. The process was quick. The words were clouded. Approval was the only word he hung to. After forty-seven years behind steel bars Mendoza would be allowed to leave. Elation was followed by terror. Out there things had changed, he gathered this from television. People spoke into phones while they shopped for groceries. Cars dictated directions. The blue glow of computers illuminated family rooms instead of television sets. Mendoza was escorted to the gates. He wore clothes that were given to him by an organization that would oversee his rehabilitation. The cane that he used to walk pressed firmly into ground that was not encased in wire. A nephew he had never met picked him up and offered to give him a home. On the drive to this new home Mendoza watched the road, and the shops they passed. Shopping malls had turned into these giant fortresses of commerce. Banks had shrunk down into small squared blocks. Mendoza asked to be driven to the bank, at Milwaukee and Diversey, if it still existed. Mendoza's nephew confirmed that it did. Inside, Mendoza shuffled in. A man in a white shirt and black slacks asked him if he needed assistance. Mendoza said no. Instead, he took a seat in the waiting room, and waited for his younger self to walk through those doors, where he would demand money in the most unpleasant of words and where he would spray bullets in the most reckless of ways. He looked down at his gnarled hands and wondered if he would recognize himself.

The plot

The Romans did not count the days of the month in consecutive numbers.
The Romans instead counted backwards from three fixed points; the
Nodes, the 5th or the 7th of the month, the Ides, the 13th or 15th, and the
Kalends, the first of the following month. The Ides of March marked
the feast of Anna Perenna, the goddess of the new year. The observance
showed aspects of the ancient Greek pharmakos ritual, the beating of an
old man in animal skins, driving him from the city. This ritual symbolizes
the expulsion of the old year. At the theater on this Ides of March we
encounter Ista quidem vis est! Cesar in this final act of violence was stabbed
23 times. Shakespeare wrote Et tu, Brute? Cesar lay on the Senate floor,
where he fell, for nearly three hours before his body was carried away.
Before he died he called out Kai su, teknon?

You too, child?

History is repeated, in variations. Centuries later, after the Roman general
died by the hands of those he loved and loved him, others fall. In Mexico,
this night, high in the mountains, a man recognizes a godson of his. He
says to his godson, the similar words, words that are not to be read, but
that should be heard "Eres tu?" The man dies, and even though he does not
know he has died he knows that this scene will be repeated again.

The witness

There's a small shop in the hills of Catalonia. It's pushed back away from where the sun will strike it. The windows are covered in a thin layer of dust, just thin enough that you can still see through the glass, but you realize that this place is aged, slowly freezing into a time that no longer exists. The miracle maker sits at his worktable, fashioned of heavy wood and lined with small instruments that require great care and great skill in use, but will, one day soon, be packaged in a box where they will sit unused for so long that they will be tossed to make way for new things. The miracle maker pulls a sheet of metal across his work table. He looks at the smooth surface and wonders what it is he can fashion with this material. It is Friday and so he believes today is a good day to make hearts. He will cut small hearts, making over 100 out of a sheet a yard wide. He bends over the metal, and using a pair of scissors with a black handle he proceeds to cut. A wind travels through his shop and the thousands of metal miracles chime like a dream catcher. Part religious and part folklore, these tiny metal acts of devotion are offered up to the heavens, up to the saints. These metal plates are reminders of petitions, for those in need, for those in prayer, and for those seeking gratitude. At one point, they would focus attention to a specific ailment, someone with an injured foot could leave a small *milagro* of a foot at a saint's shrine. The miracle maker stops cutting out the heart, small shapes that would have once been used for people to request prayers for healing for a heart condition, love, or another condition, and he sets his scissors down. The man walks to the door, looks out of the smudged window of time, and flips the sign to read out "CLOSED." People no longer care for miracles, he thought. Then he turned off the light.

Amoras anticipation

Your eyes remind me of a Prague afternoon
Royal mile espresso burns my tongue
Reminiscing of a dream we both had in Mexico
Dusty towns and clouded hopes
A sinkhole leads to turquoise waters
Riddles of jewels of those sacrificed
Starbursts when we realize
We've both been here before
Footprints fading in this jungle
Where jaguars played
Where warriors were slayed
This all dissolves into mountain mists
Abundant memories collected
Fossilized years burned your fingers
Laughter brings you to me

Jactancia de quietud

Stars assault the darkness, more profound than unidentified strips of light
This tall, morphing city, she has stolen the countryside
I'm sure these streets will taste my blood, and I observe those who will be
    my murderers
I can't understand them.
They wrestle with emptiness, yet speak of value
They speak of joy, but rot with cancer
Smiles are papier mâché cracked shells
Time lives without them
They are recyclable humans, unworthy of tomorrow as they waste their today
I move slow, because I come from so far away, and I expect no one to
    welcome my arrival

Manuscrito hallado de un libro de Joseph Conrad

Child of Apollo and Ewa, and Berdichev
Nets of Victor Hugo and William Shakespeare
Windows closed, and glass shattered across the summer day
Fevered coastlines, and dazzled
Hearts forged of Darkness

Ivory coasts and ancient nights lay at the end of the ocean
Waters overflowed and limits awakened
Stars were crossed and canoes sunk
A man marks time with his cigar

Uncoiled snakes stretch across constellations
Past, present, it's all the same
Barbarianism versus civilization, I see
Man of all men

Adrogue

The man took to the center, alleviating all breath from
Circumstance. His skin was worn with travel
of hazardous walls and London's Towers
Dialog misplaced and forgotten at the accent

A raven steps across the crumbling stones
This plutonian bird turned its head, listening
for Odin's news, curiosity piercing our souls
No one will fear the arcane night

Emblematic worlds. Pupils water colored in a
Dull afternoon. There is no time here, it was eaten
By the dead, hungry for recollections
My steps feel old as they disappear into the ground

The sleeping bird flaps its wings, its eyes closed
For the blindness is painful. This is life's chessboard
Visions casting shadows and those asleep ignoring
Doors that open to yesterday and tomorrow's death

Lions tell us stories, tales that never left us
At night, the tiger stalks our bedroom waiting for
Disruptions in sleep. This man is the accumulation of
His years, faded imprint on a mirror's glass

Years as his staff. The classroom before him takes
Objects presented in foreign words and I'll think of
Your Argentine twilight, those Buenos Aires streets
Imagine the crowds, vibrant and wonder risen

Stripes camouflaged in concentric circles, lines defined
In ambiguity, as the water drips, each ping against the

Cynthia Pelayo

Metal sink is another thousand twilights, wasted and ignored
Underutilized and coated in years wasted

Stinging in his myopia. Before his pupils, he wonders if this
is the constellation or a Labyrinthine dream.
Thoughts are calculated in mathematical dimensions
Measured in proportions only the blind comprehend

Like he said, "The first chapter is common to all…
Those who read in chronological order (e.g., x., y., z.,)
will miss the strange book's peculiar flaws.
By nickname you may call him this.

Gentleman Pri Fix Samuel Beckett will give you a nod
Visit at Saint Andrews. Slow perceptions gave worth
to those things you were able to see.
Summarize your Spanish, English, French, German and English

What is left are analogies Eulogized. Babel's Tower
grasps or gasped at confrontation of these stars
The faithless are grounded in the golden abyss
I open the door and you are sitting there, as you should be.

Your desk is covered in a scattered mess of ideas
Fantasies, and you're searching for something, searching
No one has the answers to the questions that you have created
Inaccessible as violets embracing Adam and his Eve

A voice as elegy, haunted where you were beloved
It's difficult to understand, to listen as these vines creep
Roses keep their secrets entombed and you cannot pass
The agony of who you are

Una rosa amarilla

On the island of Puerto Rico, in the center
The mountains are covered in a fog of unrelenting unreality
In the early morning hours it smells of mist and rain
At a small two bedroom wooden house
The porch is large enough for just a single chair,
Positioned sideways.
But still, this is enough space, for an old man to sit
And wave at passing cars
Las night, the pueblo was quiet
Because the old man was not seated at his porch
The cars still passed
Praying for a great invasion
The smell of coffee roasting
Inside the home there was a living room
Inside the living room there was a sofa
Framed pictures on the wall displayed children and weddings and babies
Cherished but unknown, these moments of their life on paper
These moments of their lives celebrated away from the vines
And the streams and the mountains that birthed the idea of them

Mi vida entera

I've come back again to this place
Immeasurable lions, entrusted to my care
I've come to you, robbed and weary
Past these stone steps, they have taken my happiness
I've been painted with a badge of suffering
I tire of this grotesque ballet
I've been in love with the living and maddened by the dead
Steeples reaching skies that will forever falter
I'll shroud my city in a thousand chandelier promises
I promise to pray to you
I promise to sleep of you
I believe you will be in my death
Of my dreams and misery
I believe my nights are your poverty and to God I am just an
Echo

Sunset Over Villa Ortega

Ashes cover the asphalt
Gun powdered illness shields their eyes
Blue and red flashes line the parade
Sorry lives here
Gutted desperation weakens
Burned grass and broken hydrants
Fiery circles, children stand watch
There are no streets here
There are only imaginings of things
Glittering skies fall to your illusions
Boarded windows, crumpled wrappers and misguided schools
Clouds stretch above at night, a parade of specters
Bullets pepper over playground swings

Cynthia Pelayo

Las cosas

This page. That letter. Those keys.
Coins in jars. Dried roses hung. A cracked porcelain mug.
Few days are felt and fewer are left to me and still I find no time
Filtered afternoon digested through a never-ending haze
So many things riddle my life
Fewer things make sense in obscurity
Fabrics and plates, structured piles of communications
Blinded by want, ignorant of need
Material breaks, discarded
Wasted understanding of what was necessity

La pesadilla

I think of them, those men that sailed across a world
In mounted vessels of silver and iron. Their withered
Beasts waited in the bowels, for the moment when their
Hooves would yet touch the comforted surface of land
That man, the one with the red beard, with shards of gray,
Silver and gold. He sets foot on the beaches, gilded crosses
Surround him. Looks of bewildered ancients before him
Confusion has never struck such a people so violently
This was a grave trip that now challenges
the world that still challenges me from me,
and my own bitterness, and my stolen family gaze
When day breaks I will still be unsure if that man
Is gone, or if he ever will be gone

Cynthia Pelayo

El remordimiento

My crime, is that I have never been satisfied,
Nor will I be with what I have been given
With what I have been handed, yes a mother's life
And a father's dedication, but I wanted infinitesimal
Knowledge of the museum, the pages of Alexandria's
Library, the magical ability of Shakespeare's Three Witches
The Gothic Power of Edgar Allan, the logic of Einstein.
My apologies are recited only to make you feel better
I'll never feel better, unattended and inattentive because I could
Not acquire those pages
I could not bring that brilliance, beaming
Apologies to my parents
I am a dreamer

A un gato

Mirrors will not guard your secrets
Nor will shielding your face from the rough glass
The tigero raised his dagger, mahogany cast the image
Which cannot be distorted, but can be misguided
Time is not linear, language is inconsistent
We are all divine, decreed by Queen Isabella
At the foot of Ghandi's cremation my toes crushed marigolds
This solitude, majestic of solitudes careless wonders
Wrapped in infinity, and misplaced on the journey
Wasted and asthmatic, I'll forget you
My love left me, insulted by my hand
I'll live in this world, and your reality will run parallel
Our worlds face one another but will never touch

Yo (I)

Polished bone within a warm chest
Because of this blood I will be held back from knowledge
I'll fantasize of my flaming inferno, and the Old Man of the Sea
As called by Homer, tell me my future or I will capture you
Skeletons line the ocean floor and I see those blue specters
Weeping for the memory of the bursting sun
Crimson and gold, radiating possibility and then fading into
Nothing. I see the ships reaching for shore and I see how they
Disappeared into the pages of books, pages burned
I'll mark the pages of the dead and outline their disasters of
Sunsets and burials and funeral hymns of a black cat
They failed to hope before they could cease to live
Gold-leaf, leather bound words
Time we never thought would end
The man sits and reads, in an empty house void of words

Elegia de un parque

The labyrinth wrapped around eternity
It twisted and reflected, a memory of that place
Where laughter was carried across blocks
Fighters turned, tossed, and colors blurred, reds and yellows
Violets as bells, that lined the walkway, and on the wall,
In the center of the room, a clock protected by a metal chain
Was trying to escape our childhood? It would burst
From its edges. The scent of something refined and lost, the idea
Of that temperature is lost to me now. The trickle of a sprinkler
Once gushed with pride, this is where they belonged
For us there was nothing greater
What we were when we were there. The guilt of childhood cannot
Be forgotten. It stings my throat and I choke on those tears
It was a past that cannot be revived because we had already vanished

Cynthia Pelayo

Sala vacia

The gilded mirror is fake. Its trim made of plastic.
The sofa, the loveseat, equally are covered in plastic,
Clear sheets. On the white wall, a section is faded,
This is where the oil painting of the Nina, the Pinta
And the Santa Maria rested for years, before
Time was spent here, in inescapable winters
And unrelenting summers. Spring fed basements
Fall ushered in societal expectations of educations
The house seemed so dark then, wood trim and
Creaking stairs, leading up and down, to these rooms
Cracked statues of saints tucked in the corners of this home
Seated there, at the window, looking out and hoping
No one would look at you. You spoke of street cars and
Boarding houses, of how things once were without
Saying that things were never going to be again
It will always smell like that Sunday afternoon
Sadness coated in your tone, knowing you were fading
You were now the ancestor

Curso de los recuerdos

My memory of that summer afternoon, walking down a then safe block
Past buildings and homes and a garage facing the street, the door pulled back
To show childhood fantasies of polished bikes and those in states of repair
But still, they meant freedom

From my window, I shouted your name, and you opened yours and we would
Sit against our window sills, and talk of things of little value to us now
But those minute challenges were our life, and I knew you would be there always
When the violets died I knew you were gone

Adolescent laughter is free from sin, and it was no sin the mischief we raised
Singing against the sunrise, beating our drums and our symbols, waking
    neighbors
Life was fresh, and all was grand in this military hall, and we would live
    like this forever
Until we no longer could live like this

We were taunted together, pricked and poked, mocked and kicked, blood
    ran in classrooms
Counselors and advice stifled very little of the anger and anguish and
    complicated years
The days morphed as they do, and you chose your path and my path chose me
We're so different now and my heart hates that

Those years were insomniac. Pots of coffee, packets of cigarettes and
    emergency room visits
For anxiety and stress. The diagnosis, panic. Books littered my bedroom
    floor, and places
Not mine. Nights serving people plates who would always look at me as a
    server and not anything valuing of any degree

I did not want to love you and so instead you loved me. Leave me alone, I said, but instead

You followed, concerned by my rage, promising to ease the frustration and
to stay

Years have passed and each time I tell you to leave you won't. You're here, still.

I resent you, because if you would have let me leave I could have had the world

We called it the last meal, sitting in your father's inner city apartment while
he made us all

Noodles. "This is the last time we're ever going to be in the same room,"
one of us said

That was so many years ago, and it's true. You've come and gone, and you
both hate us

Your father now is entombed in eternity, but I see him still there, cigarette
in hand and smiling

Punching keys, and flickering monitors, and endless streams of words that
mean very little

That very little I value, and the manic flow of these demands makes me
wonder if this is what I

Should have been suffering for, losing friends, dying of panic, and
exhausting my eyes

My pupils sting from sitting here and they burn back anger that this is life

Hiding my want of things, ignoring the tiger pacing the inner halls, and
the cold steel

My mind is ramblings of desires, and curses of misdirection, Where are you
going? What

Have you done? Is this the meaning of this? I wake in the morning lost in
these decisions

Regretting it all and unsure anything can be replaced

No eres los otros

You are not those competing powers tattooed in black ink
Unintended in their angled distractions. Their words, ideas
wrapped around whims and fortunes are not Yours
Your footprints haven't yet been placed, to be discovered
Instead, you're listed in the manual of those to be ignored,
rejection slips, Jesus' anguish cannot ease your suffering.
Ghandi's words cannot alleviate self-destruction. Take the stage,
Do not fear the harsh lights, nor the empty seats. It smells of
age here, but you're brimming with wonder, words will be
Written on your lips, and spun gold by the Fates.
God awaits your cries tonight, from your ten by ten room
Your pen is larger than your heart so use it, wielding the tragic end
Wrapped in a blanket of tear-stained stars, you are reckoned
Seconds are all you really have to make your next move

Los enigmas

I'm speaking to you, these very words now. I'm listening to my voice
Tomorrow morning I will be dead. When the moon rises sharply
Tomorrow afternoon I will be drained, my organs divided
Two nights from then, family will hold my wake, my funeral
My burial. In death, I am magic, and not bound to reality.
My rules are realms of wonder. Let the tarot reader read your cards.
If you fear the images she will read your palm. Heaven and hell
have locked their gates to me. They have phoned and told me to keep
Away. Purgatory does not exist. I've been banished to the labyrinths, the world
Of puzzles, where riddles make the weak weep. Lightening flashes in my
    darkened eyes
I've lived only for the adventure of living but now you tell me to experience
    an empty death
What do others experience? Can they lay down in the watery worlds? Why
    am I underserving?
You've kept me, never knowing, never worthy, drinking in this hopeless
    colored oblivion
Tomorrow it will be as if I have never breathed

A quien ya no es joven

Harsh rays of the sun pressing against your dry cheeks
Moonbeams tucked within the fine lines at the corners of your eyes
Stiff neck and legs pierced with pain remind you of that run, that fall
Dark veins winding across palms, and swelling within fingers
Gray streaked hair reminders of the color of tombstones
Faded pictures in plastic frames of people who no longer call
Dried flowered memories collecting dust of moments all of forgotten
Except you, you cling on, panicked and hopeful of youth's return
Cycles of the Earth, one, two, three, how many years have there been
Four, five, ten, thirty-two, fifty-nine, memory lapses and the fog stretches in
In between that night we laughed at the planets and our chests were
Filled with brilliance and destinations, but now we've faded. We'll no longer
Hike those rivers or take that plane, or sign passport applications. Our
Opinions are disvalued, irreverent and irrelevant. Those dreams have self-
    destructed.

El instante

Hundreds and thousands of years have led us to this moment
Can the specters of saints and knights see their product? Can they agree?
This is where we are, with more words than items cracked and bruised with
    memory
Thirteen silver coins, a wooden cup, a sword of kings held only by kings,
    these are wisps

Today is teetering and fragile. Today is your yesterday, their history
Lucky are those who have pages honoring them in books, wicked are those
    that did nothing
Born one year and died another, nothing left to commemorate an idea
Clocks are nightmares, and years are the monsters

From the rooster's crow to the dog's howl is endless
Hours in between hold sickness, suffering, death and birth
Cracked mirrors give us distorted moments, wrenched from meaning
At night, our reflections sing to us their demon songs and their angel's cries
Right here, right now, this is your heaven and this is your hell

El reloj de arena

Salvador Domingo Felipe Jacinto Dali i Domenech's
Memory persists. When you were five, your mother whispered
"You are a reincarnation." Thought to be death made flesh
 and blood again, more than a resemblance but a child lost

A copy, with a different reflection of a corpse's image
Portrait of My Dead Brother, is an optical illusion of the fascination
You named the first Salvador, and so the second was an imagination
A reawakening, the doppelganger, and far from original, or so you say

Dark hair transforms into the black plumes of a crow
Attempts at eradicating the brother fail, for constant comparisons
Of a deceased sibling reincarnated in Lichenstein's dots
Parent's bow over their child's coffin painted by Millet

When you placed your hand inside your jacket pocket
Did you feel it, did it sting? Charred flesh, scent of a charnel
House. Cloth and shoes, cotton, silk, leather, a woman's scarf
A man's handkerchief, monogramed initials, flames took that too

Thin gold chain, attached to your waistcoat, an umbilical cord
to time. A pocket watch decay, time melts us, dragging us down
away from the minutes whose hands are monitored by the monster
that cannot move, cannot speak, eyelashes unblinking

Ants crawl across the landscape seeking seconds, eating the past
Preventing the present, and we are all translucent things
Our dreams sink in a font of boiled Holy Water
Your creation is a composition of reflected heat

The clock maker is sitting at his table, planning who is next
He has awakened from a dream, where you are trapped in a

Labyrinthine world. He observes your panic, but he cannot
Understand the day this all fits, or the night that it must be

When you sleep the Earth continues its slow progression through
The galaxy, capturing glass, and stars, dust and nightmares
The scene is set at Cap de Creus. Trees don't grow here, this isn't the
Place for patience. Winds beat, creeks wind into the sea for Hercules

And the sand contained in that scene, or stilted time
Are we each a grain, an element so small, immeasurable by any hour?
Time will move us but she does not compromise, you cannot move time
It never stops and you are weak for wishing a reflection on a moment

A living thing trapped in an uncontrollable cycle
Fortunes and sorrows quantified by sickness, illness, anxieties
Sand is infinite and our lives are not, distorted wonders
Inexplicable drowning in lacks of pleasure

When a moment has passed, do you realize it? Did you see
It's right there? You are the present reflection of the past
No moment is repeated and we fear retreating into misdirection
Your future mirrors actions that are untrustworthy

Why do we reach for devices of time? Seconds morph
A breath rests, but air struggles to find its meaning
I will wind you, set you, and listen for your alarm and when
You sound, I will ignore you, close my eyes and defeat you

God reaches for the hand, and dusts off the glass, the numerals
Are brilliant black, and I'm watching the sand, the grains fall
On my face, filling my eyes, nostrils, and mouth, you say
Listen, and tell me to wait for a moment unreturned

Borges y yo

I instructed the taxi driver to slow down. He raised his eyebrow. I could see that in the rearview mirror. Midday traffic in Buenos Aires nearly consumed Borges, but I found him, walking, going somewhere, someplace. I had discovered Borges in the Garden of the Forking Path. Thereafter poems came, letters, more ficciones. I continued finding his name in letters, in books, in aging newspapers. There were other interests I followed, of course. Locating antiques of the early 20th century - typewriters, letter blocks, fountain ink pens, black and white photographs, postcards, and a sampling of taxidermy. I searched through your interviews, hazy recordings dubbed and recorded, uploaded to internet pages, a web you would never come to understand. There was your blindness, your intellect, your grace, and a love and expertise in literature; Ancient and English, yet boldly Argentinean. I read about your father, his love of writing, but his lack at becoming widely read, your sister Norah, the bullies at school, the family trips; moving across Europe, educated in Switzerland. You believed in the magic of tigers, father told you to hold the dagger in your hand. You slipped into your world, of labyrinths and night. You spoke of blindness, of the other. You covered mirrors, for fear of seeing a reflection other than your own. And I followed you, through your streets, in the heat of the Argentinean sun. I drove through suburbs of mythologies, lectures of Whitman, and drank English literature. This is Borges' game and I am in it, with you. I am trapped in your eternity, my life for an escape. I have lost everything to infinity. Oblivion justifies actions to no one. These pages are my salvation, and Borges's words breathe. I rest in my fate, in my writing to you. Recognizing that I don't know who wrote this, either Borges or me.

La lluvia

The smell gives warning that it's time to recollect
It's fresh, a scent from the heavens, of childhood and of
Hope, layered with sadness because we have all cried
During a summer's rainfall

We can all remember the celestial water falling on our
Crown, eyes rolled upward to the heavens, arms outstretched
The eagle's familiar, deep breath or air and water and you
Say the name, the only name that will ever matter

It taps on the windowpane, awaiting your admission inside
Pewter clouds stretch across your roof, wrapping vines of
Grapes across your home

Your steps have been showered by the evening
A voice comes through the rain
It is death

Mexico

An eagle perched atop a cactus, eating a snake
Prophecy ordered your direction, to a vast kingdom
Gilded in shimmering desert sand. Men on horses, crosses covered
In blood. Latin turned Castilian turned Spanish
Vaqueros and courtyards, prickly flowers of the dessert
Catrina and her smile, death with its hold
Still, you smile with a song in your heart, and daylight
In your eyes, slow and churning, loving your moon
Never forgetting your myths and gods, flickering candles
On the nightstand, Virgin Maria, Virgen de Guadalupe
Ballads are sung in the square at night
Church bells ring across in the morning
Saint Pedro and Saint Miguel hang from your neck
You are eternal

El Borges

Borges writes the night, pen listing objects of eternity
Thoughts mixed with fine ink and this is the man
Who gifts us an idea, of stretched planes, crossing into
The other, crashing ancestral heroes, and tigers made
Real for our dreams, His speech is exact, confident
Calculated, and precisely the sound that the oceans
Make when they crash into the edges of our mind
This is the Borges, a man, an enigma, an idea possessing
Of art and mind, Eastern treasures and the South American
Heart, but an English soul that rests comfortably now
Fantasizing of endless rows of books filled with beasts
And wonder, heroics and mystics, imagination bursting
And a present meant to live in the past, but we are living
Yet, you speak to me in the future. Are you here with me now, Borges?

El Punal

A dagger is hidden in a house

You will likely find it in the wooden cabinet. Look in the top drawer, and carefully move your hand to the rear. You will feel its sheath. Don't be afraid. The dagger cannot kill you. As you hold it in your hand now it is at your service.

Throats of tigers have been slashed with this cold blade. As you see, it's sharp and clean now. The blood has been wiped off. Stories tell of men that have been killed with this same blade. Human blood spilled for power.

The dagger in your possession is a tool to kill.

Steel forged for the purpose of protection. Yet, the dagger has killed and will kill. As all blades were made to wound, puncture, and slice. Lungs pierced. Throats slit. Stabs of assassination. This point has been driven into the flesh of Jesus and Cesar. It will continue to kill, because that is of its nature.

Slide the blade back carefully in its casing. Open the top drawer once again, and lay the dagger to rest. Allow it to sleep, in the cool comfort of the dark cabinet. It will remember you.

Pity the murderer as you mourn the dead. Years will pass but killings are daily.

Una brujula

No secrets remain
Translations have answered all queries
Indecipherable words sketched out on pads
Your rushed historic presentation

Paris, Budapest, Krakow, and Prague
Everyone in my life failed to see my despair
Cobblestoned steps lead me to the beginning
Multiple languages offered no clarity

Names inscribed on tombstones have been doctored
Shadows appear across mausoleums beckoning us
To correct the typos

Cardinal points escaped from a dream
North, South, East, West – suddenly I slipped into
Your sleep and you were dreaming of escape

A quien esta leyendome

I apologize for my guilt. Panic stricken sickness
Gnawing at my heart. My words feel heavy in my head
They're heavier on the page. I'll ask for your forgiveness
But I fear you may not hear me. I can't speak. I prefer to hide.
Wet ink is the only scent I can register. My fingers are locked in
A perpetual state of production, because my mind hurts the thoughts
Are so rapid and I need the text on the page to communicate my
Fears. If the fears are written then I am free but if I am free you are damned
And this is just a recording, an image and sound, because I am dead
Read my tombstone, date, month and year, reduced to numbers, a calculation
A stock epitaph tells nothing of the life bled – but it makes family feel better
My life, because I've never mattered. I've tried, fought, and only then could I
Step up on the curb from the street and look up at the twilight, knowing
I've come here unwanted, misguided, and alone except for the pages in my hand

A una moneda

My father placed you on my palm
At school my face was threatened
I remember how you placed them,
Carefully, all you had and nothing
More. We were nothing but we did
Not require anything more, a glint
Of light shown from my dresser. I
Lifted the coin to my eyes and it showed
Me the trials of the universe, boundless
And infinite. Sleep and awake,
I held my sight carefully feeling no
Remorse for this incarnation I was handed
Flesh made life, and a coin lost in time

Al hijo

It was not I who ushered you in, it was the dead
A line of fathers, uncles, grandfathers – men who
Weakened and died long before the idea of you
Was born. You are Adam's son, a part of the great
Mythology of this world. You were born of love and
Bred of magic. Folk tales and lore, and legend
You are who we are and who those were before me
You are a sampling of the line, yet, present in the past
You are their reflection, my reflection, and your sons
To come will see their image in the dawn and this
In my image you will find the knowledge of those
Before, but you will be free from their road
In love you will grow, a future of brilliance
Enchanted in our eternal labyrinth

Cynthia Pelayo

Fragments from an Apocryphal Gospel

Wretched are the poor for their spirits will not be mourned on Earth.

Wretched are those that weep, for their tears leave crystal cuts on flesh.

Lucky are those that suppress their suffering, for pain is a sin.

It is not enough to hide. For you will be found hiding in your place of failure.

Happy is he who remains intent, resigning into his position of unimportance. Your thoughts are unwelcome.

Happy is he who shuns others. For they do not belong in our Old Testament.

Blessed are the meek. For their tongues have been bound, and their fingertips have been burned.

Blessed are those who hope for justice. For they know their cries were silenced the moment it touched their lips.

Blessed are the merciful. For their work will go punished and their challenges will be many.

Blessed are the pure of heart. For they will hear the voice of God over loud speakers.

Blessed are those who suffer persecution. For their fight is an endless tangle of misplaced truths.

Your blood is the salt of the Earth, sprinkled across desserts and asphalt.

Let the light of one lamp be lit. Only the blessed will see it.

Every commandment is broken by men.

He who kills for any cause is the sinner of all men.

Acts of men are worthy of brimstone

Do not hate your enemy. For if your mind is focused on them you will never be free from them.

Forgive the offenses. You will be divided from it.

Do not make lies the cult of truth.

Do not survey paths for their proclaimed untruths.

Revenge and forgiveness shall not be unfiltered. They belong to our apocalypse.

Doing good for your enemy services only your humanity.

Do not accumulate material wealth on Earth. Items wither and rot.

Believe that others are just as they are and you are as you are and neither will ever meet at an intersection of understanding.

God measures men in riddles only answered by His guardians.

Give your gold, your food, your money, your time to the weak and weary. They have only dreams.

Seek for the pleasure of seeking. There is no other pleasure.

The path not chosen is the inaccessible path.

Do not judge man for his works. He is capable of other things.

Nothing is built on stone. We're all crashing through clay and landing on dirt.

Happy are the poor without serenity and the rich without their heart.

Happy are the brave, who accept their fate of...

Happy are those who hold memories of man's Son.

Happy are those who live to love and love living with the pain of having loved.

Happy are those who are happy.

Nostalgia del presente

At this very moment I am thinking
Of those times and of that joy
With you, and I feel ill, disconnected
From the present because I long to
Breath in another year when laughter
Sounded different and the sun glowed
Just slightly stronger, and night was
Bursting with radiance and my heart
Is so heavy, weeping of that time that
I am suddenly there

About the Author

Cynthia (Cina) Pelayo is an International Latino Book Award winner. She is the author of Loteria, Santa Muerte and The Missing. Pelayo holds a Master of Fine Arts from The School of the Art Institute of Chicago and is a Phd candidate at the University of Illinois at Chicago in Hispanic Literary and Cultural Studies. She lives in Chicago with her husband and son.